Animal Spikes and Spines

Beaks

Rebecca Rissman

 KU-655-460

www.raintreepublishers.co.uk
Visit our website to find out
more information about
Raintree books.

To order:
☎ Phone 0845 6044371
🖶 Fax +44 (0) 1865 312263
✉ Email myorders@raintreepublishers.co.uk

Customers from outside the UK please telephone +44 1865 312262

DUDLEY PUBLIC LIBRARIES

L

735870   Sch

J598.2

Raintree is an imprint of Capstone Global Library Limited,
a company incorporated in England and Wales having its
registered office at 7 Pilgrim Street, London, EC4V 6LB
– Registered company number: 6695582

Text © Capstone Global Library Limited 2011
First published in hardback in 2011
The moral rights of the proprietor have been asserted.

All rights reserved. No part of this publication may be reproduced
in any form or by any means (including photocopying or storing
it in any medium by electronic means and whether or not
transiently or incidentally to some other use of this publication)
without the written permission of the copyright owner, except in
accordance with the provisions of the Copyright, Designs and
Patents Act 1988 or under the terms of a licence issued by the
Copyright Licensing Agency, Saffron House, 6–10 Kirby Street,
London EC1N 8TS (www.cla.co.uk). Applications for the copyright
owner's written permission should be addressed to the publisher.

Edited by Daniel Nunn, John-Paul Wilkins, Rebecca Rissman,
and Sian Smith
Designed by Joanna Hinton-Malivoire
Picture research by Tracy Cummins
Production by Victoria Fitzgerald
Originated by Capstone Global Library Ltd
Printed and bound in China by Leo Paper Products Ltd

ISBN 978 1 406 22421 4 (hardback)
15 14 13 12 11
10 9 8 7 6 5 4 3 2 1

British Library Cataloguing in Publication Data
Rissman, Rebecca.
Beaks. -- (Animal spikes and spines)
1. Bill (Anatomy)--Juvenile literature.
I. Title II. Series
591.4'4-dc22

Acknowledgements
We would like to thank the following for permission to reproduce
photographs: Getty Images pp **15** (Jill Flynn), **17** (Nancy
Nehring); istockphoto p **6** (© Joe Gough); naturepl.com pp **13**,
14 & **23b** (all Rolf Nussbaumer); Photolibrary pp **11** (Thomas
Sbampato), **12** (Sylvain Cordier), **18** (Chad Ehlers), **20**
(Imagesource), **22** (Thomas Sbampato); Shutterstock pp **4**
(© Johan Swanepoel), **5** (© Robag), **7** (© Francois Loubser), **8** (©
Vivid Pixels), **9** & **10** (both © Eduardo Rivero), **16** (© gary718),
21 (© Despot), **23a** (© Eduardo Rivero), **23c** (© Despot).

Cover photograph of a great white pelican (Pelecanus
onocrotalus), reproduced with permission of National
Geographic Stock (Mike Lane/ Foto Natura/ Minden Pictures).
Back cover photograph of a keel billed toucan reproduced with
permission of Shutterstock (© Eduardo Rivero).

We would like to thank Michael Bright, Nancy Harris, Dee Reid,
and Diana Bentley for their assistance in the preparation of
this book.

Every effort has been made to contact copyright holders of
material reproduced in this book. Any omissions will be rectified in
subsequent printings if notice is given to the publisher.

DUDLEY SCHOOLS
LIBRARY SERVICE

Schools Library and Information Services

S00000735870

Contents

Animal body parts

Animals have different body parts.

beaks

Birds have beaks.

What are beaks?

beak

Beaks are hard, sharp body parts.

Birds use beaks to do many things.

Different beaks

Beaks can look very different.

Beaks can be many different colours.
What bird is this?

This bird is a toucan. It uses its beak
to reach for food.

Beaks can be wide and flat.

What bird is this?

This bird is a shoe bill. Its beak is
shaped like a shoe!

Beaks can be long and narrow.
What bird is this?

This bird is a hummingbird. It uses
its beak to drink from plants.

Beaks can be pink and black.
What bird is this?

This bird is a flamingo. The food it eats makes it look pink.

Beaks can have bumps.
What bird is this?

This bird is a Chinese goose. It uses its beak to eat seeds and plants.

Your body

Do you have a beak?

No! Humans do not have beaks.

Humans have teeth to help them
to eat.

Can you remember?

Which bird's beak is shaped like a shoe?

Picture glossary

 **beak** the hard, pointy parts of a bird's mouth

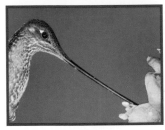 **narrow** thin or short from side to side

 **teeth** hard body parts used for biting and chewing

Index

Notes for parents and teachers

Before reading

Show children the front cover of the book. Guide them in a discussion about what they think the book will be about. Can they think of some ways that birds use their beaks? List their ideas on chart paper. Discuss how beaks are body parts and the way in which animals can use their beaks to do different things.

After reading

- Reference the chart that you created before you read the book. Ask children if their predictions about the ways birds use their beaks were true.
- Group the children into pairs. Ask the children to take turns to act out one of the ways that a bird might use its beak for their partner to guess.